The HIPAA Roadmap for Business Associates

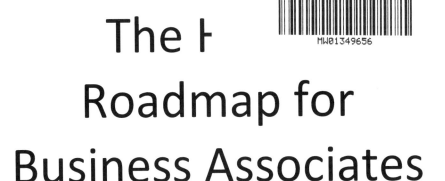

A step-by-step guide to HIPAA/HITECH compliance

By Patricia D. King, J.D., M.B.A.

Disclaimer: The HIPAA Roadmap for Business Associates is intended as general information and guidance and does not guarantee compliance with federal or state laws. The information presented may not be applicable or appropriate for all business associates, as individual circumstances may vary. The HIPAA Roadmap for Business Associates is not intended as an exhaustive or definitive source of compliance guidance and does not constitute legal advice. Consult a licensed attorney for legal advice applicable to your situation.

©2013 Digital Age Healthcare, LLC

Contents

Introduction 1
Who is a Business Associate? 3
How to Use the HIPAA Roadmap for Business Associates 5
1. Step 1 – Getting Ready 7
    1.1   Understanding HIPAA Security 7
    1.2   Understanding the Breach Notification Rule 8
    1.3   Understanding Your Other Responsibilities Under HIPAA 9
    1.4   Appoint your Security Official 10
        Document 1: Security Official Job Description 12
2. Step 2 – Surveying the Landscape 15
    2.1   Identify your existing policies relating to privacy and security of health information 15
    2.2   Assess your information security risks 15
        Document 2A: Initial Risk Analysis Checklist 18
        Document 2B: Information System Inventory 21
        Document 2C: Inventory of EPHI 23
        Document 2D: Inventory of Threats and Vulnerabilities 24
    2.3   Mind the gaps! 26
        Document 2E: Sample Documentation of Choice of Security Measures 27
    2.4 Contingency Planning 28
        Document 2F: Contingency Plan Checklist 30

3. Step 3 – Planning the Route 34

   3.1   Adopt information security policies 34

      Document 3a: Security Official Handbook 36

      DOCUMENT 3B: Staff HIPAA Security Handbook 71

      Document 3C: Employee Sanction Policy 75

   3.2   Adopt a Breach Notification Policy 76

      Document 3D: Breach Notification Policy 77

   3.3   Adopt a Policy on Compliance with the Privacy Rule, Including the Minimum Necessary Standard 82

      Document 3E: Policy on Compliance with the Privacy Rule 83

Step 4: Start Your Engines 84

   4.1   Staff Training 84

      Document 4A: Staff Training 85

   4.2   Amend Your Business Associate Agreement 102

      Document 4B: Business Associate Agreement 103

      Document 4C: Business Associate Agreement Amendment 112

   4.3   Amend Your Agreements With Subcontractors 114

Step 5: Handling Bumps in the Road 115

   5.1   Security Incidents and Breaches 115

      Document 5: Security Incident Report 116

Appendix A: Other Resources 117

Appendix B: Definitions 118

THE HIPAA ROADMAP FOR BUSINESS ASSOCIATES

INTRODUCTION

The Health Insurance Portability and Accountability Act (HIPAA) was enacted in 1996. HIPAA's main purpose was to allow employees covered by a group health plan to continue coverage for a period after ending their employment, and to receive credit for prior coverage when enrolling in a new group health plan. HIPAA also included "Administrative Simplification" provisions, intended to make insurance claims processes more efficient by requiring standard identifiers for employers, health plans and providers, and establishing uniform code sets for standard transactions.

When we think of HIPAA today, our first thoughts may be of the privacy and security provisions of HIPAA. These provisions were included in the Administrative Simplification section of HIPAA, reflecting the judgment that if health information were to flow more freely from providers to payers and among other components of the health care industry, the privacy and security of consumers' protected health information (PHI)[1] should be protected under federal law. Compliance with the HIPAA Privacy Rule was required beginning in 2003, and the Security Rule in 2005. Both the Privacy Rule and Security Rule are administered by the Office of Civil Rights (OCR) of the Department of Health and Human Services (HHS).

Originally, the HIPAA Privacy Rule and Security Rule had direct application only to "covered entities", defined as health plans, health care providers that submitted electronic claims, and health care clearinghouses.[2] However, both the Privacy Rule and Security Rule affected business associates, because covered entities were required to include provisions protecting the privacy and security of PHI in their contract with business associates. When the American Recovery and Reinvestment Act, commonly called the stimulus law, was enacted, parts of HIPAA were applied directly to business associates. The stimulus law included a section called the Health Information Technology for Economic and Clinical Health (HITECH) Act. Under the HITECH Act, key provisions of the HIPAA Security Rule and the civil and criminal penalties for HIPAA violations apply directly to business associates. Also, if the business associate is responsible for carrying out some of the responsibilities of the covered entity, relevant provisions of the Privacy Rule also apply directly to the business associate. The HITECH Act also mandated new rules requiring covered entities and business associates to notify affected individuals and HHS when there is a breach of unsecured[3] PHI.

On January 25, 2013, the final rule implementing the HITECH Act and making additional changes to the HIPAA Privacy Rule, Security Rule, Breach Notification Rule and Enforcement Rule were published in the Federal Register. With publication of the final rule, there is now a firm deadline for business associates to comply with the HITECH Act requirements: **September 23, 2013**. Business associate agreements in force at the time of publication are grandfathered for one year, provided that the agreements met the original HIPAA standards. By the end of that year, all agreements must be modified as necessary to comply with the final rule.

Now, you as a business associate can be audited for compliance with the Security Rule, the same as covered entities. You have independent obligations to report breaches of unsecured protected PHI just as covered entities do. Now it is more important than ever that you understand what you need to do to protect yourself from the substantial fines and adverse publicity that would follow from violation of the HIPAA rules.

WHO IS A BUSINESS ASSOCIATE?

A business associate may be a business performing functions that necessarily involve the disclosure of PHI, such as claims processing, utilization review, billing, quality assurance, or benefit management. Companies performing other types of services, such as legal, accounting, financial, or administrative services, may also be business associates if they need to have access to PHI in order to perform their tasks. For example, a law firm that provides malpractice defense for health care providers will be a business associate, because the firm will need access to the medical records of claimants in order to represent their clients. On the other hand, a firm providing legal assistance in negotiating business contracts will not likely be a business associate. Similarly, a consulting firm that analyzes coding and billing practices for health care providers will be a business associate, while a firm advising on marketing strategy will not be.

Someone who performs services involving access to PHI, who is part of the workforce of a covered entity, is not a business associate. For example, while a company that provides software maintenance services for electronic health records will usually be a business associate (assuming the company will periodically need access to PHI to fix software bugs), if the company provides service by locating one of its employees on the premises of the health care provider, that employee may be considered a member of the provider's workforce rather than a business associate.

Companies that only transmit information without accessing it (such as delivery services), or may access information only incidentally (such as a janitorial service or copy machine repair services) are not business associates. Also, a health care provider acting in its capacity as such is not a business associate. For example, when a physician sends PHI to a laboratory so that the laboratory can perform tests and report the results back to the physician, the laboratory is acting as a health care provider and not the physician's business associate.

As you can see from this brief description, many types of businesses may be business associates. Here are examples (not an exhaustive list):

Accreditation organizations

- Billing companies
- Collection agencies
- Companies performing data conversion, de-identification or data analysis involving PHI
- Data destruction companies
- Health information organizations, including health information exchanges and e-prescribing gateways
- Patient Safety Organizations
- Record storage companies
- Vendors of personal health records (if the personal health record is offered on behalf of a covered entity)
- Subcontractors of business associates
- Utilization review organizations

How to Use the HIPAA Roadmap for Business Associates

The HIPAA Roadmap for Business Associates consists of a set of tools: worksheets, forms, model policies and other tools that you can use to implement the HIPAA Security Rule for your company, comply with the Breach Notification Rule, and meet all other requirements of HIPAA that apply to business associates. It is organized in a functional manner. For example, while the Roadmap is designed to help you comply with all 18 standards and 36 implementation specifications of the Security Rule, it is emphatically not just a set of 54 policies. Some of the standards call for development of policies, and to comply with those standards and implementation specifications, the Roadmap includes model policies. But to comply with other standards, the company must carry out a particular task (such as conducting a risk analysis, or assigning responsibility for the security program to a designated person). For these tasks, the Roadmap includes checklists, forms and other tools to help you complete the required activity.

Consistent with its functional orientation, the HIPAA Roadmap for Business Associates is designed to lead you step by step, in logical sequence, through the tasks you need to accomplish to comply with HIPAA. Step One is to appoint your Security Official, since that person will be responsible for assuring that the other steps in the process of complying with the HIPAA Security Rule are completed. Step Two is to conduct your risk analysis, because the policies and other elements of your security management program must be based on the findings of your risk analysis. As you proceed through the rest of the steps, you will be gradually building an effective, compliant information security program and establishing the policies and forms you need to comply with HIPAA.

Establishing and maintaining an effective information security program is not only a regulatory requirement, but also a critical activity for the protection of your customers' information. Your customers expect you to handle their patients' information with the same care that you devote to your own confidential information. As health care information increasingly moves from paper to electronic media, different tools are required to protect patient privacy. Using the HIPAA Roadmap for Business Associates, you can craft an effective information security program suited to the needs of your customers and their patients.

---

[1] The term "individually identifiable health information"(IIHI) is defined in the regulations as health information that relates to an individual's physical or mental health, provision of health care, or payment for health care, that either identifies the individual or there is a reasonable basis to believe the information can identify the individual. This is closely related to the term "protected health information" (PHI), which excludes IIHI contained in educational records and employment records.

[2] Health care clearinghouses process the claims submitted by providers into formats compatible with the claims processing systems of various payers.

[3] PHI which is encrypted is not considered unsecured. For this reason, encryption (especially on mobile devices) is an important step to consider to avoid liability under the breach notification rule.

1. STEP 1 – GETTING READY

1.1 UNDERSTANDING HIPAA SECURITY

The HIPAA Security Rule is both narrower than the Privacy Rule in one sense, and broader in another way. Unlike HIPAA Privacy, the Security Rule does not apply to PHI in paper form, but only to electronic PHI (EPHI): that is, to PHI that is maintained in electronic media, or transmitted in electronic media. EPHI includes PHI in computer memory, including mobile devices such as tablets and smartphones; and also PHI stored in digital media, such as CDs or thumb drives.

Like the Privacy Rule, the Security Rule requires you to protect the confidentiality of EPHI. But there are additional obligations under the Security Rule: you also must protect the integrity and availability of EPHI. That is, you must assure that (1) EPHI can be accessed when needed to provide services (e.g., your system is not down when needed to perform critical functions, and there is a backup plan to allow operations to continue during unscheduled downtime), and (2) that your policies and systems protect against unauthorized alteration of EPHI.

You need to conduct a risk assessment of vulnerabilities of your EPHI, and then implement "reasonable and appropriate" safeguards. What is "reasonable and appropriate" depends on several factors, including your organization's size and technical capabilities. For example, more will be expected of a large health information exchange with an Information Systems Department than of a billing company with five employees. In most cases, smaller business associates can meet this requirement by adopting common-sense information security measures (e.g., installing antivirus and firewall software, and updating your operating system when required), implementing the security features already present in your software, and adopting appropriate policies. Larger business associates would benefit from assistance by a certified information security specialist, and this is highly recommended for more complex organizations. Business associates of all sizes should address protection of EPHI on mobile devices, since many reported data breaches have resulted from loss or theft of laptops or other devices.

The Security Rule includes both mandatory and "addressable" implementation specifications. HHS has made it clear, however, that "addressable" does not mean "optional". It just means that there are multiple ways of meeting the standard, and you should adopt the measures appropriate for your organization.

The HIPAA Roadmap for Business Associates will take you through the steps needed to implement reasonable and appropriate safeguards to protect your EPHI. Larger business associates may also want to check out the additional resources linked at the end of this publication.

1.2 UNDERSTANDING THE BREACH NOTIFICATION RULE

The Breach Notification Rule applies to both HIPAA covered entities and business associates. When there is a breach of unsecured PHI, notice must be given to both the individuals whose PHI was compromised, and to the Office for Civil Rights (OCR). "Unsecured PHI" means PHI that has not been encrypted. Many reported breaches have involved loss or theft of laptops and other mobile devices. To minimize these foreseeable risks, therefore, it is important to encrypt PHI on mobile devices and strictly control when mobile devices may be used to store or access PHI.

An impermissible use or disclosure of unsecured PHI is presumed to be a breach, unless the covered entity or business associate demonstrates that that there is a low probability that the PHI has been compromised. This is determined through a risk assessment, including at least the following factors:

- The nature and extent of PHI involved, including the types of identifiers and, in the case of PHI which has some identifiers removed, the possibility of re-identification
- The unauthorized person who gained access to PHI
- Whether the PHI was actually acquired or viewed
- The extent to which the risk to the PHI has been mitigated.

If there is a breach, notices must be sent to all the affected individuals. If there is a breach involving 500 or more individuals in an individual state, OCR must be notified within 60 days. The covered entity or business associate must maintain a record of breaches involving fewer than 500 individuals, and report all such breaches to OCR annually.

The business associate agreement between you and a covered entity will also require that you report breaches to the covered entity, and may specify a timeframe shorter than the 60 days so that you and the covered entity can jointly evaluate the circumstance and determine which party will notify individuals.

1.3 UNDERSTANDING YOUR OTHER RESPONSIBILITIES UNDER HIPAA

If your services involve carrying out any of the responsibilities of HIPAA covered entities (such as handling patient requests for copies of their records), you will need to comply with provisions of the HIPAA Privacy Rule that apply to these services. For example, if you handle patient requests for their records, you will need to provide copies within the time limits set forth in the Privacy Rule (30 days, or 60 days for records stored offsite); deny requests for records only as permitted under the Privacy Rule, provide notification of denial of the request and keep records of such denials; limit charges for copies to amounts permitted under the Privacy Rule and applicable state law; and if the provider maintains all or part of the designated record set in electronic form, provide an electronic copy.

You are also required to follow the "minimum necessary" rule when you request PHI from a covered entity or from another business associate, or when you use or disclose PHI. This means using, disclosing or requesting only the minimum necessary PHI needed to accomplish the intended purpose.

Business associates also are responsible for keeping records to demonstrate their compliance with HIPAA, submitting compliance reports to OCR, cooperating with complaint investigations and compliance reviews, and permitting OCR to access their information for purpose of assessing HIPAA compliance.

1.4 APPOINT YOUR SECURITY OFFICIAL

The HIPAA Security Rule requires that you designate a specific individual to be responsible for managing the security of your EPHI. This person will analyze risks to your EPHI from internal and external factors; adopt security policies; be responsible for training your office staff in how to protect EPHI; make sure that if you have arrangements with third parties dealing with EPHI, there is a business associate agreement or subcontractor agreement with the appropriate protections; and investigate any security breaches. While the Security Official can delegate tasks to others, the "buck stops here".

Who should be the Security Official? If you outsource management of your information system, you can designate your consultant. If there is one employee in your company who is interested in health information technology and willing to assume this administrative responsibility, that would be appropriate. When you have chosen your Security Official, be sure to document that selection.

Document 1 is a job description for the Security Official capturing the duties of that individual as required in the HIPAA Security Rule.

DOCUMENT 1: SECURITY OFFICIAL JOB DESCRIPTION

Position Title: Information Security Official

Qualifications:

1. Expertise in the principles of security management relating to information systems

2. Familiarity with the structure and operation of the Company's information systems

3. Knowledge of the Health Information Portability and Accountability Act (HIPAA) Security Rule, Breach Notification Rule and relevant aspects of the Privacy Rule

Responsibilities:

1. Performs an accurate and thorough risk analysis of the Company's information systems, to assess the potential risks to, and vulnerabilities of, the confidentiality, integrity and availability of protected health information (PHI) and electronic protected health information (EPHI) held by the Company. Updates the risk as appropriate to respond to introduction of new technology and changes in the environment. Recommends and implements security measures sufficient to reduce risks and vulnerabilities to a reasonable and appropriate level.

2. Develops and implements policies and procedures to prevent, detect, contain and correct security violations.

3. Regularly reviews records of information system activity, such as audit logs, access reports, and security incident tracking reports.

4. Develops and implements policies and procedures to ensure that employees of the Company have appropriate access to EPHI as needed for their job functions, and that access to the Company's EPHI is denied to persons who are not authorized to access that information.

    a. Implements procedures to require that persons who work with EPHI or in locations where it resides must have authorization, or be appropriately supervised.
    b. Implements procedures to determine what access to EPHI should be granted to individual employees. Grants access privileges to individual programs, transactions, workstations, processes, or other appropriate categories. Documents access privileges. Periodically review access privileges and modifies as appropriate.
    c. Implements procedures to terminate access to the Company's EPHI when an employee leaves the Company.

5. Implements a security awareness and training program for all employees. The training program will include initial training for all employees joining the Company; training updates to alert employees to changes in the Company's security policies; and security updates and reminders as needed. The training will include procedures for creating, changing and safeguarding passwords; reporting of security incidents; safeguards to avoid introducing viruses, worms and other harmful code; and other rules for safeguarding the Company's EPHI.

6. Regularly monitors attempts by unauthorized persons to log on to the Company's information system.

7. Implements procedures to guard against and detect viruses, worms and other malicious code.

8. Develops and implements policies to respond to security incidents, including procedures to mitigate harmful effects of a security incident, and to investigate and document security incidents.

9. Develops a contingency plan to respond to emergencies that cause system failure, loss of data, or corruption of data. This must include a data backup plan; disaster recovery plan; and procedures to continue critical operations during an emergency. The contingency plan be tested periodically.

10. Performs periodic technical and nontechnical reviews of the Company's information security program.

11. Evaluates reports of incidents that may involve breach of unsecured PHI. Performs a risk assessment of each such incident to determine whether PHI was potentially compromised. Reports breaches of unsecured PHI in accordance with the Breach Notification Rule.

2. STEP 2 – SURVEYING THE LANDSCAPE

2.1 IDENTIFY YOUR EXISTING POLICIES RELATING TO PRIVACY AND SECURITY OF HEALTH INFORMATION

You may have existing written policies and procedures for protection of PHI held or transmitted by your company. Gather any existing policies relating to computer security, release of health information, granting employee access to EPHI, employee discipline for improper disclosure or security breaches, and other procedures relating to protecting confidential information.

2.2 ASSESS YOUR INFORMATION SECURITY RISKS

Your Security Official's first task should be to perform a comprehensive risk analysis of your electronic information system. This includes several tasks:

- Collecting system-related information, including identifying system hardware, software, interfaces (internal and external connectivity), storage media, and users;

- Compiling a complete inventory of where the Company's EPHI is stored, and how and where EPHI is transmitted;

- Identifying risks to the system from external and internal sources;

- Assessing the system's vulnerability to the risks;

- Identifying existing security procedures and safeguards;

- Recommending additional security controls (including technical controls, physical security measures, and administrative procedures; and

- Documenting the risk assessment process.

The time and resources required to perform a risk assessment will depend on the complexity of your information system. The Security Standards mandate an "accurate and thorough assessment of the potential risks and vulnerabilities to the confidentiality, integrity, and availability of electronic protected health information." The requirement for a risk analysis is meant to be "scalable" to the resources and individual requirements of the organization.

As you conduct your risk assessment, be sure to consider all of the following:

Your physical plant

Are your offices secure from intrusion at all times, 24/7/365? Are areas within your offices that house computer systems and sensitive information secure even from unauthorized employees, by separate locks or other means to restrict access? If you share office space with other companies, have you prevented them from accessing your EPHI through physical or technical barriers? Have you taken steps to protect EPHI in the event of a natural disaster, through off-site storage or other means?

Your servers and computer system

If EPHI is stored on your own server, do you have redundant or back-up systems? If EPHI is stored in the "cloud", do the service arrangements prevent other customers of the cloud computing service from accessing your data, and do you have appropriate privacy and security protections in your agreement with the cloud computing service?

Communications

When you transmit EPHI, you must use a secure method such as transfer to a secure site with data encrypted during transmission.

Mobile devices

Loss or theft of mobile devices is a very significant risk to the security of EPHI. Generally, EPHI on mobile devices should be encrypted unless there are barriers to using encryption that cannot be reasonably overcome. If you decide that it is not feasible to encrypt data on mobile devices, be sure to retain a written record of the reasons why you have reached this decision.

Documents 2, 2a, 2b and 2c are designed to help you review potential vulnerabilities of your information system in a systematic manner. These forms follow an approach adapted from guidelines of the National Institute of Standards and Technology (NIST) publications on information system security. The documents in this section will help guide your risk analysis process, and generate the required documentation. Be sure to customize them to your specific needs. Also, be sure to include everything used by your Company to hold or transmit EPHI, whether located at the office, at an employee's home, or offsite. Retain the completed documents for at least six years as evidence of your risk assessment process.

DOCUMENT 2A: INITIAL RISK ANALYSIS CHECKLIST

GENERAL OFFICE ITEMS	YES	NO
1. If your office is in a high crime area, do you have a physical security system?		
2. Do you have a log listing every person who has been issued a key to the office?		
3. Do you document return of keys when a person is no longer employed or contracted?		
4. Do you share office space with unaffiliated companies?		
SOFTWARE ITEMS		
1. Is your operating system still supported by the vendor?		
2. For any computer with Internet connection, have you installed firewall software?		
3. Have you installed anti-virus software?		
4. Have you installed anti-spyware software?		
5. Do you use the monitoring features of your software to periodically review access to data?		
WORKSTATION ITEMS		
1. Is a log-in routine required for access to any workstation?		

2. Are your workstations located in high-traffic areas, where they may be seen by customers, members of the public, etc.?

3. Do you use an automatic logoff function?

4. Do you require that screensavers activate after a brief period of inactivity?

BACKKUP ITEMS

1. Do you routinely back up your EPHI to backup tapes or other media (CDs, etc.), or use cloud-based backup?

2. If you backup to tapes or other media, are your backups stored offsite or in a secure location (e.g., a fireproof safe)?

3. Are your backups immediately available (e.g., on a non-networked computer) if your system is down?

4. If your backups would not be immediately available, do you have other means of getting immediate access to critical information (e.g., paper backups)?

WORKFORCE ITEMS

1. Does each employee and other workforce member (e.g., on-site contractor) have a unique login ID?

2. Have all workforce members received security training including protecting the confidentiality of passwords, proper use of email and the internet,

and security of mobile devices?
COMMUNICATION ITEMS
1. Do you transmit data files containing EPHI only to a secure site?
2. Do you prohibit emailing EPHI, or if you permit it, do you require encryption?

DOCUMENT 2B: INFORMATION SYSTEM INVENTORY

HOW TO USE THIS DOCUMENT: This document will help you identify all elements of your information system, and begin to identify gaps in information system security. For each item checked, review information in the Comments column. For any No answer, this suggests a potential gap that will need to be addressed.

COMPONENT	Included in your system?	COMMENTS	Yes	No
Servers				
Dedicated servers		Are frequent backups performed?		
Shared servers		Does the host segregate data of different customers? Are frequent backups performed?		
"In the Cloud"		Are frequent backups performed? Is there an uptime guarantee?		
Software		Is access restricted to appropriate users?		
		Are backup copies of software programs maintained?		
Devices		Is there a comprehensive inventory of devices that may contain EPHI?		
		If employees are permitted to use their own devices (smartphones, laptops, tablets), are employees required to follow your		

	security policies for these devices?
	Is there a system for tracking which employees have access to employer-owned devices?
	If EPHI is on mobile devices, is it encrypted?
	Is there capability for remote data wipe if the device is lost or stolen?
Data storage	Are there procedures for data back-up, and prohibiting deletion of data?
Users	Is access to EPHI controlled by user ID and password?
	Have all users received information security training?

DOCUMENT 2C: INVENTORY OF EPHI

HOW TO USE THIS DOCUMENT: This document will help you identify all EPHI you maintain or use, and identify appropriate users. In the second column, check all that apply. Use the Description/comments column to record significant information, such as name of software, etc. List job titles of users in the last column.

Location of EPHI	√	Description/comments	Users
On workstations			
On laptops			
On smartphones			
On tablets			
On employee home computers			
In third party databases			
Embedded in medical equipment			
Other			

DOCUMENT 2D: INVENTORY OF THREATS AND VULNERABILITIES

HOW TO USE THIS DOCUMENT: This inventory lists threats and vulnerabilities common to most information systems. Use the priority column to designate those threats that you have experienced, or which you consider most likely or most significant. For the threats you have identified as priorities, use the last column to designate whether or not you currently are utilizing a means to control the threat.

Type of threat	Priority ✓	Examples of tools to control risk	Risk control utilized
ENVIRONMENTAL THREATS		PHYSICAL SAFEGUARDS, ADMINISTRATIVE SAFEGUARDS	
Earthquakes, tornadoes, hurricanes, floods, etc.		Offsite backup	
Fire		Fire retardant, offsite backup	
Power outages		Auxiliary power supply, downtime procedure	
Chemical spills and other pollution		Offsite backup	
OUTSIDE HUMAN THREATS		TECHNICAL SAFEGUARDS, PHYSICAL SAFEGUARDS	
System penetration		Firewall	
Hacking		Firewall	
Information theft		Privacy control software	
Viruses, worms, etc.		Antivirus software	
Spyware		Firewall, antivirus software	
Website			

jamming/denial of service attacks	
Spam	Spam filters
Theft or destruction of hardware or devices	Locks, facility security system, inventory control, encryption of EPHI on mobile devices
INSIDE HUMAN THREATS	**ADMINISTRATIVE SAFEGUARDS, TECHNICAL SAFEGUARDS**
Browsing EPHI	Password protocols, access restrictions, monitoring
Deletion of data	Disaster recovery
Unintentional	Training
Deliberate	Authorization/supervision, termination procedures
Input of wrong data	Training
Misdirecting email	Training
Information theft	Authorization/supervision, termination procedures
Viruses, worms, etc.	Security training
System sabotage	Authorization/supervision, termination procedures
Software malfunction	Downtime procedures

2.3 Mind the Gaps!

The HIPAA Security Rule requires you to protect against any reasonably anticipated threats to the confidentiality, integrity and availability of EPHI. The regulations permit you to use any security measures that allow you to "reasonably and appropriately" implement the Security Rule. You need to take into account the following factors:

- The size, complexity, and administrative capabilities of the Company;
- The Company's technical infrastructure, hardware, and software security capabilities;
- The costs of security measures; and
- The probability and criticality of potential risks to EPHI.

In this step, you will address gaps identified in your risk assessment. If you completed Document 2, Initial Risk Analysis Checklist, you need to address each item where you answered "No". In most cases, you should take the step necessary to change your "No" to a "Yes". However, in some cases, there may be valid reasons not to take this step. If so, you should include the rationale in your HIPAA compliance documentation. If you completed Documents 2, 2a, 2b and 2c, review the information you collected through this step to identify security measures that can contain risk to your EPHI. This includes the gaps identified in Document 2a, Information System Inventory. You should also include those threats and vulnerabilities identified as priorities in Document 2c, Inventory of Threats and Vulnerabilities, if you are not currently using a risk control mechanism to contain the threat. Remember to document the rationale for the choices you make.

DOCUMENT 2E: SAMPLE DOCUMENTATION OF CHOICE OF SECURITY MEASURES

The following are two examples documenting the reason for implementing a security measure:

Example 1 (gap identified in Document 2a):

In the course of our risk analysis, we noted that the Company uses Windows 2000 on some desktop computers, and this operating system is no longer supported by Microsoft. Security patches are no longer published by Microsoft for this version. Therefore, we have decided to upgrade to Windows 8. Cost will be $_____, and estimated implementation date is _____.

Example 2 (threat identified in Document 2c):

Because the Company is located in a high-traffic area, there is a significant risk that computer equipment could be stolen after business hours. Neighboring offices have experienced thefts of office equipment. Therefore, we have decided to install a security system. Cost will be $_____, and estimated implementation date is _____.

The following example demonstrates documentation of a company's choice not to implement a security measure:

Example 3 (threat identified in Document 2c):

We identified that we could lose access to our computerized patient billing system if there were a power outage. We have used surge protectors to protect against momentary power fluctuations. We considered implementing a battery backup system to supply power during more extended outages, but concluded that the cost of this option exceeded the expected benefit. Power outages are rare in our area. We will prepare for the contingency of a power outage by requiring regular backups of our patient billing files, and developing a downtime procedure until the system is restored.

2.4 Contingency Planning

Even if you do a thorough risk analysis, and implement technical solutions and policies to help you minimize risk, there will still be some "residual risk". That is, there will be some unavoidable circumstances that could cause you to temporarily lose access to your EPHI. The purpose of contingency planning is to anticipate how you will handle this type of circumstance, so that your operations are disrupted as little as possible. According to the HIPAA Security Rule, contingency plans should address assessment of the priority of various information systems; data backup; disaster recovery; emergency mode operation; and periodic testing of your contingency plan.

Your contingency plan will be incorporated in Section 8 of the Security Official Handbook. To guide you in customizing these policies for your practice, complete the Contingency Plan Checklist that follows.

Document 2F: Contingency Plan Checklist

Part 1: List your information systems containing EPHI and determine their priority.

Consider which systems most directly affect your ability to deliver critical services; these should be given priority. Since your operating system is fundamental to all of your other systems, usually this should be recovered first,

System Name	Priority
Operating system	1
Internet access	
Email	
Software program #1	
Software program #2	
Office programs (word processing, spreadsheets, etc.)	

Part 2: Data Backup and Recovery.

For your critical information systems that contain EPHI, determine what media you will use for backup (e.g., saving data to CDs, or to a network drive that is backed up automatically; or printing out information on paper). Determine how often the data will be backed up (e.g., nightly for critical information, or weekly for less critical). Then decide where the back-up media and installation software for your programs will be stored (e.g., office safe for backup CDs of critical information, offsite storage for long-term preservation, etc.). Finally, if the data is lost, determine how it will be recovered. For example, if your network is down, do you have a non-network computer that could be used for temporary access to data until the data can be reinstalled on the network drive?

Complete the following table to document your data backup and recovery plan. The entries in the table are examples only; be sure to customize this for your operations.

Software/Data	Backup Media	Frequency of Backup	Location
Licensed programs	Original installation CD	N/A	
Customer data	Cloud server; backup tapes; CD	Daily	
Smartphone data	Backup to main computer system	Daily	

Part 3: Continuing Operations While Recovery is Underway

Consider how you will respond if your information system is down due to an emergency. If the emergency affects your complete operations (e.g., fire, flood, etc.), you will need to notify staff. If this is more than a few individuals, consider compiling a "call tree" and make sure all managers have a copy at home.

If your office is operational but your computer system is down, your staff will need to temporarily document on paper and transfer the data to your system when function returns. Think about how you will handle requests for data while your system is down.

Complete the following form to document your disaster recovery plan. Again, the examples given are suggestions only.

DISASTER RECOVERY PLAN

1. If the office must be closed:

    - Implement call tree. Responsibility: _____
    - Notify outside parties: _____

2. If the computer system is down:

- Document on paper. Enter documentation in the system when normal function is restored.

Part 4: Testing and Revision

When you have completed your contingency plan, and on a regular basis thereafter, test whether the plan actually works. For your data backup plans, test whether you can recover data from storage. If you encounter conversion problems, this gives you an opportunity to work with your vendor to learn how to accomplish a successful recovery. It may not be possible to perform an actual test of your disaster recovery plan, but you can periodically test whether your staff understands their responsibilities if it is necessary to invoke the plan.

Use the form below to document the initial and periodic testing.

Contingency Plan Test Date	Observations	Corrective Action

3. Step 3 – Planning the Route

3.1 Adopt Information Security Policies

There are, of course, many different ways to organize your information security policies. You need to bear in mind that to fully comply with the Security Rule, there are some complex tasks that must be the responsibility of your Security Official, while all employees will be responsible for following basic procedures to protect the security of EPHI. Therefore, the HIPAA Roadmap for Business Associates organizes the Security Policies into two main groups: policies which are to be implemented by the Security Official, and are included in the Security Official Handbook; and policies which must be observed by all employees.

The Security Official Handbook contains the policies needed to establish and maintain the HIPAA information security program. These policies are designated as either REQUIRED or ADDRESSABLE. For the required policies, the Company must assure that the POLICY statement is met, although the individual procedures that the Company uses to meet that standard may vary from those contained in the PROCEDURE section. The Company has more flexibility in implementing the addressable policies (but remember, addressable does not mean optional). The Security Official should take steps to achieve the goal of the policy, based on what is reasonable for the individual circumstances of the Company.

The policies that must be communicated to and observed by all employees who use EPHI are contained in the general policies. These are organized into a HIPAA Security Handbook. This could be a freestanding document, or included in a general staff handbook. In any case, remember that anyone who access EPHI must receive training on your HIPAA Security policies.

Finally, as part of this step, review any personnel policies or handbook sections dealing with employee termination procedures. It is advisable to modify this policy or statement to include a description of sanctions for violating the Security Policies. A sample policy is included.

DOCUMENT 3A: SECURITY OFFICIAL HANDBOOK

Table of Contents

I. SECURITY MANAGEMENT PROCESS AND AUDIT CONTROLS
Policy 1.1   Risk analysis
Policy 1.2   Risk management
Policy 1.3   Information system activity review and audit controls

II. WORKFORCE SECURITY
Policy 2.1   Authorization or supervision of workforce members who work with or in proximity to EPHI
Policy 2.2   Workforce clearance procedures
Policy 2.3   Procedures for terminating access to EPHI

III. INFORMATION ACCESS MANAGEMENT AND ACCESS CONTROL
Policy 3.1   Access authorization
Policy 3.2   Access establishment and modification; unique user ID
Policy 3.3   Emergency access procedure
Policy 3.4   Automatic log-off procedure
Policy 3.5   Transmission security, encryption and decryption

IV. PROTECTING EPHI FROM ALTERATION OR DESTRUCTION
Policy 4.1   Integrity and authentication

V. SECURITY AWARENESS AND TRAINING
Policy 5.1   Security training
Policy 5.2   Security updates
Policy 5.3   Protection from malicious software
Policy 5.4   Log-in monitoring
Policy 5.5   Password management

VI. WORKSTATIONS, DEVICES AND MEDIA
Policy 6.1   Workstation use and security
Policy 6.2   Device and media controls
Policy 6.3   Facility security

VII. SECURITY INCIDENTS
Policy 7.1   Security incidents

VIII. CONTINGENCY PLAN
Policy 8.1   Contingency plan
Policy 8.2   Data backup
Policy 8.3   Disaster recovery
Policy 8.4   Emergency mode operation plan
Policy 8.5   Criticality analysis
Policy 8.6   Contingency plan testing

IX. PERIODIC EVALUATION OF SECURITY POLICIES
Policy 9.1   Periodic evaluation of security policies

Policy 1.1   RISK ANALYSIS
REQUIRED

POLICY

The Company will conduct an accurate and thorough assessment of the potential risks to and vulnerabilities of the confidentiality, integrity, and availability of electronic protected health information held by the Company.

PROCEDURE

1. The risk analysis will include a thorough inventory of the Company's information system, including components of the system (hardware, software, interfaces, etc.); system and data criticality; system and data sensitivity; functional requirements of the system; security architecture; network topology; information storage protections; technical, management and operational controls; security environment; and environmental security.

2. The Company will systematically review potential risks to its information system from the natural environment (floods, storms, etc.), the man-made environment (power failure, pollution, fire, etc.), and human threats (including unintentional errors, and deliberate actions such as network based attacks, malicious software, and unauthorized access to electronic protected health information).

3. The risk analysis will identify potential vulnerabilities, and address potential losses which could occur if security measures were not in place, including unauthorized uses and disclosures of electronic protected health information; corruption of data integrity through improper modification; and disruption of availability of electronic protected health information to data users. System security testing may be utilized if reasonable and appropriate to thoroughly assess system vulnerabilities.

4. Written findings and recommendations will be recorded.

5. The risk analysis will be updated when there are significant changes in the Company's information system, environment or known risks.

REFERENCES
45 C.F.R. §§ 164.308(a)(1)(i), 164.308(a)(1)(ii)(A)

Policy 1.2 RISK MANAGEMENT
REQUIRED

POLICY

The Company will implement security measures sufficient to reduce risks and vulnerabilities to the confidentiality, integrity and availability of electronic protected health information to a reasonable and appropriate level.

PROCEDURE

1. Vulnerabilities identified by the Company through the risk assessment process will be prioritized and evaluated according to the threat posed to the confidentiality, integrity and availability of electronic protected health information, and the criticality of the data potentially affected.

2. Controls identified in the risk assessment process to contain risks to electronic protected health information, and other available controls, will be evaluated, considering the feasibility and effectiveness of the available options. Technical, management, and operational security controls may be considered, singly or in combination. Examples include:

> (a) Supporting technical controls, including unique identification of users, processes and information resources; cryptographic key management; system security; and system protections, such as residual information protection, least privilege, process separation, modularity, layering, and minimization.

> (b) Preventive technical controls, including authentication controls (such as passwords, personal identification numbers, tokens, and digital certificates); authorization controls; access control enforcement (including discretionary access control [DAC] or mandatory access control [MAC]); nonrepudiation; and protected communications, including data encryption methods such as virtual private network and Internet Protocol Security [IPSEC] Protocol, and deployment of cryptographic technologies (e.g., Data Encryption Standard [DES], Triple DES, RAS, MD5, secure hash standard, and escrowed encryption algorithms).

(c) Detection and recovery technical controls, including audit controls, intrusion detection and containment, proof-of-wholeness control, restore secure state, and virus detection and eradication.

(d) Protective management security controls, including maintenance of system security plans, personnel security controls, and security awareness and technical training.

(e) Detection management security controls, including periodic system audits and ongoing risk management.

(f) Recovery management security controls, including maintenance of a continuity of operations plan and incident response capability.

(g) Operational security controls, including physical access control; facility security; regular data and system backups; off-site storage; and environmental security.

3. Controls that are potentially feasible and effective will be further analyzed through a cost-benefit analysis. The analysis will include the impact of implementing, and of not implementing, the new or enhanced controls; costs of implementation; and assessing implementation costs and benefits against system and data criticality.

4. The Company will select controls that are reasonable and appropriate, and implement the selected controls in timely fashion.

REFERENCES

45 C.F.R. §§ 164.308(a)(1)(i), 164.308(a)(1)(ii)(B)

Policy 1.3 INFORMATION SYSTEM ACTIVITY REVIEW AND AUDIT CONTROLS
REQUIRED

POLICY

The Company will implement procedures to regularly review records of information system activity.

PROCEDURE

1. Review of access reports

    a. The Security Official will use the monitoring features present in the Company's information system to record access to the information system. If possible with the Company's information system, the Security Official should establish logs to automatically record each time a person logs in to the system by identifying the user, date, time and file accessed.

    b. If possible, the electronic access log should flag any attempt by a user to access a restricted file that the user is not authorized to access.

    c. The Security Official will review the electronic access log on a regular basis (at least weekly). If a workforce member has tried to access a file that the user does not have authority to access, the Security Official will discuss this with the individual or his/her supervisor.

    d. The supervisor is responsible for determining whether the attempted access was inadvertent or deliberate, for appropriate follow-up with the user, and for appropriate sanctions in the event the user has intentionally or carelessly violated access controls.

2. Review of audit logs and security incident tracking reports.

   a. If possible in the Company's information system, the Security Official will enable monitoring settings to automatically maintain audit trails of unusual events, such as failed user authentication attempts, changes to users' security information, error messages, and other security-relevant events.

   b. The Security Official will review audit logs on a regular basis (at least weekly) and is responsible for investigating unusual events or patterns.

3. Automated tools

   a. The Company may use automated monitoring tools as indicated by the risk analysis to detect security problems (such as virus scanners, checksumming, password crackers, integrity verification programs, and system performance monitoring).

   b. The Security Official will review output of monitoring tools on a monthly basis and is responsible for investigating unusual events or patterns.

REFERENCES

45 C.F.R.§§ 164.308(a)(1)(i), 164.308(a)(1)(ii)(D)

Policy 2.1 AUTHORIZATION AND/OR SUPERVISION OF WORKFORCE MEMBERS
ADDRESSABLE

POLICY

No workforce member may be permitted to access electronic protected health information unless access is determined to be necessary to perform the job function, and is appropriately authorized.

PROCEDURE

1. A workforce member may receive a password to access electronic protected health information only with the authorization of his/her supervisor. It is the responsibility of the supervisor:

> (a) to verify that access to electronic protected health information is necessary to perform the job, and that the workforce member's access is limited to the minimum necessary electronic protected health information necessary;
>
> (b) to ensure that the workforce member receives training with respect to safeguarding the security and confidentiality of electronic protected health information;
>
> (c) to ensure that the workforce member signs any confidentiality agreement or other undertaking required by the Company to document the workforce member's commitment not to disclose the password; and
>
> (d) to address any instances of password misuse by the workforce member.

2. Certain workforce members who are not permitted access to electronic protected health information work in areas where electronic protected health information may be accessed (e.g., maintenance workers). The Company shall take reasonable and appropriate steps to limit opportunities by such workforce members to access electronic protected health information, such as reminding employees who use the

information system to log off before they leave work and cleaning staff arrive.

REFERENCES

45 C.F.R. §§ 164.308(a)(3)(i), 164.308(a)(3)(ii)(A)

Policy 2.2 WORKFORCE CLEARANCE
ADDRESSABLE

POLICY

The Company will take reasonable and appropriate measures to verify that persons entrusted with access to electronic protected health information may be safely trusted with such access.

PROCEDURE

1. Prior to granting a workforce member access to electronic protected health information, the supervisor must examine prior work history to verify that the workforce member has not been subject to discipline for violation of confidentiality, or other significant infractions which cast doubt on the workforce member's character or professionalism.

2. Reference checks will be required for all new employees who will have access to electronic protected health information. This will include written or telephone contact with one or more of the prospective employee's former supervisors to verify the individual's reputation for trustworthiness and professionalism.

3. Workforce members who will have direct responsibilities for security of the Company's information system may be subject to additional clearance procedures, in the discretion of the Security Official. This may include criminal background checks, credit checks, and other appropriate measures.

REFERENCES

45 C.F.R. §§ 164.308(a)(3)(i), 164.308(a)(3)(ii)(B)

Policy 2.3 PROCEDURES FOR TERMINATING ACCESS TO ELECTRONIC PROTECTED HEALTH INFORMATION
ADDRESSABLE

POLICY

When an employee leaves the Company, his/her access to the Company's electronic protected health information will be terminated.

PROCEDURE

1. The Security Official will be notified when any employee is leaving the Company. The user ID for the employee will be terminated immediately in the case of an employee who is leaving the Company involuntarily, or without notice. For an employee who is leaving the Company voluntarily with notice, the user ID will be terminated at the end of the employee's last day.

2. An employee leaving the Company will turn in any keys, keycards and other items required for access to the Company's offices. If such items are not returned, or in the discretion of the manager, the Company will change locks as needed.

3. An employee leaving the Company will turn in any patient data maintained at his/her home, and delete any patient data maintained on his/her personal equipment (such as a laptop or mobile phone).

4. The employee's manager will notify the Security Official of any other circumstance in which a user ID should be terminated (such as leaves or suspensions).

5. The Security Official will periodically test the system for discontinuing user IDs.

REFERENCES
45 C.F.R. §§ 164.308(a)(3)(i), 164.308(a)(3)(ii)(C)

Policy 3.1 ACCESS AUTHORIZATION
ADDRESSABLE

POLICY

Only persons who require access to the Company's information system in order to perform their jobs will be authorized to access systems and programs containing electronic protected health information.

PROCEDURE

1. Employees who require access to the Company's information system to perform their job functions will be granted access and documentation shall be retained for each such employee. The individual programs that each individual is authorized to access will be designated by the employee's manager.

2. Contractors who need temporary access to the Company's information (e.g., for system maintenance and other functions) will sign a Business Associate agreement. Temporary user IDs created for contractors will be terminated when the assignment ends.

REFERENCES

45 C.F.R. §§ 164.308(a)(4)(i), 164.308(a)(4)(ii)(B)

Policy 3.2 ACCESS ESTABLISHMENT AND MODIFICATION; UNIQUE USER ID
ADDRESSABLE
UNIQUE USER ID REQUIRED

POLICY

The Security Official will administer procedures so that authorized users may access the Company's information system, and access privileges are modified as appropriate.

PROCEDURE

1. The Security Official will be notified of new employees and other workforce members who require access to the Company's information system. The Security Official will assign a unique user ID for each authorized person, and document the systems and programs that the individual is authorized to access.

2. All persons authorized to access the Company's information system will receive training on protecting the confidentiality, integrity and availability of electronic patient information, including guidelines for setting passwords.

3. If the job responsibilities of an authorized user changes so that he/she no longer requires access to elements of the Company's information system, or requires access to additional elements, the Security Official will modify access privileges for the appropriate systems.

REFERENCES

45 C.F.R. §§ 164.308(a)(4)(i), 164.308(a)(4)(ii)(C), 164.312(a)(1)(i), 164.312(a)(2)(i)

Policy 3.3 EMERGENCY ACCESS PROCEDURES **REQUIRED**

POLICY

The Company will establish procedures for obtaining electronic protected health information in an emergency.

PROCEDURE

If the Company's information system is damaged due to an emergency, so that normal methods of obtaining access to electronic protected health information are not possible, the Security Official will use any means possible to provide staff with access to electronic protected health information necessary to avoid disruption of the Company's operations.

REFERENCES

45 C.F.R. §§ 164.312(a)(1), 164.312(a)(2)(ii)

Policy 3.4 AUTOMATIC LOG-OFF
ADDRESSABLE

POLICY

The Company will require automatic log-off settings for workstations located in areas accessible to non-employees or to multiple employees.

PROCEDURE

1. Workstations in general office areas will be set to logoff the user and launch the screensaver after _____ minutes of inactivity.

2. Computers in private offices do not require automatic logoff if access to the office is restricted.

REFERENCES

45 C.F.R. §§ 164.312(a)(1), 164.312(a)(2)(iii)

Policy 3.5 TRANSMISSION SECURITY, ENCRYPTION AND DECRYPTION
ADDRESSABLE*

POLICY

The Company will not send patient information over the Internet unless there are safeguards to assure that patient information is kept confidential and protected from modification during transmission.

PROCEDURE

1. The Company may send patient information over the Internet to a secure site (such as a secure clearinghouse site).

2. The Company may send patient information over the Internet (e.g., through email) if the data is encrypted.

REFERENCES

45 C.F.R. §§ 164.312(a)(2)(iv); 164.312(e)(1); 164.312(e)(2)(i); 164.312(e)(2)(ii)

*While encryption is addressable, transmission security is a standard. If the Company does not use encryption, it must document some other means of securing data in transmission (e.g., prohibiting email to nonsecure sites). While in some cases other security measures may be appropriate, generally it is advisable to encrypt PHI. This is especially important for mobile devices.

Policy 4.1 INTEGRITY AND AUTHENTICATION
CONTAINS REQUIRED AND ADDRESSABLE ELEMENTS*

POLICY

The Company will use reasonable means to protect its electronic protected health information from errors, unauthorized modification or destruction.

PROCEDURE

1. Integrity controls: The Security Official will use security features of the Company's software to prevent against unauthorized access to the information system, and to warn of possible data contamination or unauthorized modification.

2. Authentication of EPHI: The Company will monitor errors in its electronic patient information. Repeated errors will be reported to the software vendor for correction.

3. Person/entity authentication: The Company will require that any person accessing or modifying its electronic patient information must be identified by a user ID and one of the following means of authentication: password; token (e.g. smart card); biometric identification; or combination of two of the above.

REFERENCES

45 C.F.R. §§ 164.312(c)(1), 164.312(c)(2), 164.312(d)

*Integrity controls and person/entity authentication are required. Authentication of EPHI is addressable.

Policy 5.1 SECURITY TRAINING REQUIRED

POLICY

The Company will implement a security awareness and training program for all employees, and all non-employed workforce members (such as on-site contractors). Security awareness means that every workforce member understands that he/she is expected to protect the security of electronic protected health information. Security training means that workforce members whose job requires access to electronic protected health information receive instruction on how to use the Company's information system properly, so that the confidentiality, integrity and availability of electronic protected health information is protected.

PROCEDURE

1. Basic security awareness will be included in the orientation of all new employees and other workforce members, and reinforced at the time of evaluation. As a part of basic security awareness, the workforce member will understand that protecting the security of electronic protected health information is critical to the mission of the Company, and is a job expectation for every workforce member, regardless of job category.

2. Security awareness will also include instruction on maintaining physical security of the premises (e.g., proper use of locks and the physical security system). Workforce members who do not require access to the information system will be cautioned that they may be subject to discipline if they should attempt access.

3. All workforce members who require access to the Company's information system will receive basic security training. Training will be updated when the Company changes its HIPAA Security Policies, or when there are changes to major features of the Company's information system that could affect security. Basic security training will include explanation of the policies that apply to all workforce members using the information system, such as:

- Proper use of email

- Proper use of the Internet
- Procedures for backup (e.g., saving of data to network drives)
- Prohibition on improper copying of files and programs, or loading of unauthorized programs on the information system
- Prohibition on attempting access to electronic protected health information not required for the job function
- Precautions against malicious software, and procedures to follow if the workforce member suspects that malicious software has been introduced.
- Precautions against inappropriate disclosure or compromise of PHI on mobile devices due to loss, theft, or use of the device in an insecure environment.

4. The Company will maintain documentation on security awareness and training of workforce members for at least six years.

REFERENCES

45 C.F.R. § 164.308(a)(5)(i)

Policy 5.2 SECURITY UPDATES
ADDRESSABLE

POLICY

The Security Official will provide periodic security reminders to inform workforce members of changes in policies, and to reinforce security awareness and training.

PROCEDURE

1. If the Company modifies its policies relating to information system security, written notice will be given to affected workforce members. Training will be provided for changes that have significant impact on job procedures.

2. The Company will implement appropriate security reminders to reinforce security awareness and training of workforce members, such as:

- Automatic reminder to change a password after a specified number of log-ins or designated time interval
- Messages on log-in screens reinforcing the importance of protecting data security and confidentiality.

REFERENCES:

45 C.F.R. § 164.308(a)(5)(A)

Policy 5.3 PROTECTION FROM MALICIOUS SOFTWARE
ADDRESSABLE

POLICY

The Company shall take reasonable means to protect against introduction of malicious software into its information system.

PROCEDURE

1. Malicious software means any software which, if introduced into the Company's information system, could result in loss of data, corruption of data, loss of use of one or more programs or systems, slowing of system response time, unauthorized transmission of data outside the system, or other impairment of system function. Malicious software includes, but is not limited to, viruses, worms, Trojan horses, logic bombs and spyware.

2. The Security Official will install appropriate programs on network servers to detect and disarm malicious software.

3. Training of workforce members will include precautions against introducing malicious software, including proper use of email attachments, security considerations when downloading files from the Internet, and prohibition against installation of any unauthorized programs. Workforce members will also be informed that they may not disable security measures installed by the Security Official.

REFERENCES

45 C.F.R. § 164.308(a)(5)(ii)(B)

Policy 5.4 LOG-IN MONITORING
ADDRESSABLE

POLICY

The Security Official will monitor unsuccessful attempts to log in to the Company's programs containing electronic protected health information and investigate unusual activity.

PROCEDURE

1. [Include if the Company allows remote access to electronic protected health information.] The Company will use appropriate measures to assure that remote access to its information system is available only to authorized users. This will include use of firewalls, TCP wrappers, strong authentication measures (such as encrypted or single-session passwords) and other measures as deemed appropriate by the Security Official.

2. If deemed necessary by the Security Official, the Company may conduct periodic penetration testing to verify the integrity of its security systems.

3. The information system will generate an automatic record of unsuccessful attempts to log in to programs containing electronic protected health information. If the log-in attempt appears to have originated from a person other than an authorized user, the Security Official will investigate the attempt as a security incident.

4. Authorized users who are unsuccessful in logging in to programs which they are authorized to access should consult the Security Official for additional training if required.

REFERENCES:

45 C.F.R. § 164.308(a)(5)(ii)(C)

Policy 5.5 PASSWORD MANAGEMENT
<u>ADDRESSABLE</u>

POLICY

The Company will establish guidelines for establishing and changing passwords. Each workforce member will maintain the confidentiality of his/her password.

PROCEDURE

1. The Security Official will establish guidelines for setting passwords, and assure that all workforce members receive training on these guidelines. If compatible with the Company's information system, passwords should have a required minimum length and consist of both letters and numbers or special characters.

2. Each workforce member will establish his/her password according to these guidelines. Passwords may not be shared with any other person, including another workforce member.

3. Passwords may not be posted on or near the workstation, or in any other place where they may be viewed by other persons.

4. Any person violating this policy will be subject to appropriate discipline. Refer to the Company's general policy concerning sanctions.

REFERENCES

42 C.F.R. § 164.308(a)(5)(ii)(D)

Policy 6.1 WORKSTATION USE AND SECURITY
REQUIRED

POLICY

Workstations used for accessing electronic protected health information will be located in secure locations, and procedures will be implemented to secure information on any mobile workstations.

PROCEDURE

1. Workstations will be located where data on the screen cannot be easily viewed by non-employees or other parties, or screens will be used to limit visibility to persons other than the user.

2. If a workstation is used for a dedicated purpose (such as billing only), employees shall be instructed on this limited use.

3. If a laptop is used as a workstation, password security and encryption must be used for the laptop. If the laptop is removed from the office for any reason, it should be checked out to the user.

REFERENCES

45 C.F.R. §§ 164.310(b); 164.310(c)

Policy 6.2 DEVICE AND MEDIA CONTROLS
**REQUIRED*__

POLICY

The Company will maintain records of the physical location of devices and media containing electronic protected health information, and their acquisition, disposition and reuse.

PROCEDURE

1. The Company will maintain an inventory of all computers (desktop, laptop, tablet, etc.), mobile phones, peripherals and other computer equipment that can contain electronic protected health information. The inventory will be updated when equipment is acquired or disposed of.

2. No computer equipment will be sold, donated or otherwise disposed of unless all electronic protected health information has been totally and permanently removed from its memory.

3. Storage devices such as thumb drives and CDs containing electronic protected health information (including backups) will be kept in a secure location, such as a locked fireproof filing cabinet.

REFERENCES

42 C.F.R. §§ 164.310(d)(1), 164.310(d)(2)

* Device and media controls, disposal, and media re-use are required; accountability and data backup and storage are addressable.

Policy 6.3 FACILITY SECURITY
REQUIRED*

POLICY

The Company will take reasonable measures to control physical access to areas where electronic protected health information is housed.

PROCEDURE

1. The Company will use reasonable methods to secure the office premises, including installing deadbolt locks on the main door, and secure locks on interior doors, file cabinets and other areas as needed.

2. The Company will maintain a record of persons issued keys to the premises.

3. The building and office premises will comply with current building codes. Locks, windows and doors will be promptly repaired as necessary.

REFERENCES

45 C.F.R. §§ 164.310(a), 164.310(b).

*Facility access controls are required. The implementation specifications (contingency operations, facility security plan, access control and validation, and maintenance records) are all addressable.

Policy 7.1 SECURITY INCIDENTS
REQUIRED

POLICY

The Security Official will implement an effective system for monitoring and responding to security incidents.

PROCEDURE

1. All security incidents (including those involving business partners) shall be reported to the Security Official.

2. The Security Official will be responsible for investigating all security incidents to determine the potential causes, and to recommend and implement measures to prevent further incidents.

3. The Security Official will determine whether the security incident has resulted in any unauthorized disclosure of electronic protected health information, corruption or unauthorized modification of data, or loss of data. Remedial measures will be taken to mitigate the effects of the security incident to the extent possible. This may include removal of malicious software from the information system, and reconstruction of data from back-up files.

4. The Security Official will document the investigation of the security incident, measures taken following the incident to prevent future similar incidents, and measures taken to mitigate harmful effects of the security incident.

REFERENCES

45 C.F.R. § 164.308(a)(6)

Policy 8.1 CONTINGENCY PLAN
REQUIRED

POLICY

The Company will develop a contingency plan to respond to disruption of its information system, and assure that employees understand how to apply the plan.

PROCEDURE

1. The Company has developed a contingency plan that is attached as an Exhibit to this Policy. [Attach a copy of the contingency plan.]

2. Security training will address how the contingency plan will be used if the Company's information system is down or not functioning properly for any reason.

REFERENCES

45 C.F.R. § 164.308(a)(7)(i)

Policy 8.2 DATA BACK-UP **REQUIRED**

POLICY

The Company will maintain exact backup copies of electronic protected health information so that data can be retrieved if it is lost or corrupted.

PROCEDURE

1. System data will be backed up [specify method, e.g. cloud-based backup, etc.] at least [specify daily, weekly, etc.] Backups will be stored in a secure location.

3. If backups are stored off-site, the entity contracted to transport the tapes must have established appropriate safeguards to protect the security and confidentiality of the data in transit.

REFERENCES:

45 C.F.R. § 164.308(a)(7)(ii)(A)

Policy 8.3 DISASTER RECOVERY
REQUIRED

POLICY

The Company will establish and periodically reevaluate a written plan to restore data lost through occurrence of a disaster.

PROCEDURE

1. The Company's risk analysis will identify the potential hazards which could result in loss of data, including natural threats (earthquake, flood, etc.), environmental threats (power failure, etc.) and human threats.

2. The Company's written disaster plan will prioritize critical functions that are most essential to maintaining operations.

3. The disaster plan will identify resources needed to support critical functions, including but not limited to workforce; processing capabilities; computer-based services (such as telecommunications); data and applications; and physical infrastructure.

4. The disaster recovery plan will include strategies to achieve prompt recovery of critical functions, in the event of occurrence of each of the hazards identified in the risk analysis.

REFERENCES

45 C.F.R. § 164.308(a)(7)(ii)(B)

Policy 8.4 EMERGENCY MODE OPERATION PLAN
REQUIRED

POLICY

The Company will establish written procedures to maintain the critical information systems required to support essential operations while operating in emergency mode.

PROCEDURE

1. The Company will develop a written emergency mode operation plan, which will identify resources that will be available to support essential operations while operating in emergency mode. This will include emergency access to processing capacity, and access to backups.

2. If the Company's information system is temporarily completely inoperable due to a disaster, the emergency mode operation plan shall identify means to critical functions. This may require exclusive use of paper recordkeeping until normal information system operation can be resumed.

3. The emergency mode operation plan shall prioritize functions, so that system capacity can be devoted to the most critical operations if the information system is partially inoperable.

4. The emergency mode operation plan shall identify means for accessing backups to restore system functionality.

REFERENCES:

45 C.F.R. § 164.308(a)(7)(ii)(B)

Policy 8.5 CRITICALITY ANALYSIS
ADDRESSABLE

POLICY

The Company will assess the relative criticality of specific applications and data in formulating its contingency plan.

PROCEDURE

1. Those applications and databases identified as critical to the Company's essential functions will be given priority in the contingency plan.

2. The Company will devote appropriate resources devoted to recovering critical functions in the event of disaster.

REFERENCES

45 C.F.R. § 164.308(a)(7)(ii)(E)

Policy 8.6 CONTINGENCY PLAN TESTING
ADDRESSABLE

POLICY

The Company will periodically test its information system contingency plan, and revise the plan as indicated by the results of the test.

PROCEDURE

1. The Security Official will designate a schedule for testing contingency plans on a regular basis.

2. The test will be designed to simulate potential threats to the information system from environmental and human sources, but will be conducted in a controlled environment.

3. The test will evaluate adequacy of back-up and recovery systems, and time required to return the system to a normal operating environment.

4. If the test reveals vulnerabilities or inadequacies of back-up and recovery systems, appropriate modifications will be made in the contingency plan.

REFERENCES

45 C.F.R. § 164.308(a)(7)(ii)(D)

Policy 9.1 PERIODIC EVALUATION OF POLICIES REQUIRED

POLICY

The Security Official will perform periodic technical and nontechnical evaluations of the Company's security policies in response to environmental or operational changes, and update policies as needed to comply with regulatory changes.

PROCEDURE

1. The Security Official will perform periodic evaluation of its information system components to certify the level of security. Where appropriate in light of the Company's risk analysis, certification may be conducted through an external accreditation body.

2. The Security Official will review publications of the National Institute of Standards and Technology (NIST) and industry developments to remain informed of current industry standards for information system security and the development of certified security products.

3. The Security Official will document the outcome of the certification testing, and implement changes to information system security as indicated by the analysis.

REFERENCES:

45 C.F.R. § 164.308(a)(8)

DOCUMENT 3B: STAFF HIPAA SECURITY HANDBOOK

The Staff HIPAA Security Handbook should be given to each of your employees when they receive their HIPAA Security training. Staff members do not need to have the in-depth knowledge of information security that the Security Official must have. However, all staff should understand the basic safeguards that they need to follow every day on their job.

INTRODUCTION

The privacy of our clients' patients is central to the mission of our Company. Our clients and their patients trust us to maintain the confidentiality of their health information. We honor that trust when we follow our policies that are designed to prevent inappropriate disclosure of patient information.

As the health care industry changes, more and more patient information will be kept electronically, rather than on paper. The Health Insurance Portability and Accountability Act (HIPAA) Security Standards are designed to protect electronic patient information. We need to keep that information confidential, free from errors, and available when we need it to provide services for our clients.

Every employee will receive training on the policies our Company is putting in place to protect our electronic patient information. This handbook supplements that training by providing specific answers to common questions.

Passwords

I already have a user ID. Why do I need a password too?
Your user ID is assigned to you, and could become known to and used by others. You create your password yourself, so that only you will use the system with that unique combination.

What kind of password should I use?
When you create your password, the system will tell you if you must use a minimum number of characters, if you must have a combination of letters and numbers, and if there are any characters you should not use. Choose a password that is easy for you to remember, but would not be easy for anyone to guess. Do not use consecutive numbers, the word "Password", your name, or other personal facts that are well known to your coworkers.

Why do I need to change my password?
It is a good practice to change your password from time to time to maintain its security. Do not alternate between two different passwords, but try to think of a unique new password. One technique is to think of a group of names that you will remember, such as the characters in your favorite TV show, breeds of dogs, types of flowers, etc. Then when you change your password, move to another name in that category.

Can I share my password if a coworker forgets his/her password?
No. Your coworker can get a new password by having the Security Official or office manager reset the system.

I can't get all the information I need to do my job with my password. Can I use my supervisor's password?
No. If you cannot get the information you need, ask your supervisor to authorize you to access the additional program or screen.

Security Incidents

What is a "security incident"?
A security incident is anything that could cause data loss or corruption, or cause the system to go down. This could happen from many causes. Loss of power, introduction of a virus that destroys files, or introduction of spyware that captures system information are some examples.

What should I do if I become aware of a security incident?
Report the incident immediately to the Company's Security Official. Use appropriate secure means. For example, if you suspect the email system is insecure, use the phone.

Downtime Procedures

What should I do if the system is down?
Document activities on paper. The paper documentation will be recorded in the system when operations are restored.

[Add any specific procedures you developed as part of your contingency plan.]

Use of Email and the Internet

Are there guidelines I should follow for using email?
The Company's computer system is for business purposes only; keep personal use of email to a minimum. You should be aware that email received through the Company's information system is not your personal correspondence, and like any business, the Company has the ability and legal right to monitor email use of employees.

Use precautions to protect against introducing viruses and other dangerous computer code. Do not open email (especially email attachments) from an unknown source. Do not send or respond to "chain" emails.

Can I send patient information via email?
Generally, no. Patient information can be emailed only if encrypted or sent through a secure site. Contact the Security Official or your manager if you need to send patient information via email.

Are there guidelines for proper use of the Internet?
As with email, remember that your access to the Internet through the Company's system is for business use only, and can be monitored. Also, use precautions to avoid introducing viruses or spyware. Do not click on pop-ups or other ads.

Sanctions

Can employees be disciplined for violating the Company's security rules?
Yes. Protecting the security of the Company's electronic patient information is a critical element of each employee's job. This could range

from a reprimand for an unintentional security breach, to termination for serious, intentional or repeated violations.

DOCUMENT 3C: EMPLOYEE SANCTION POLICY

The purpose of this policy is to comply with the following standard and implementation specification: Administrative Safeguard Standard: Security Management Process; Implementation Specification: Sanction Policy (Required). Integrate this policy into your general employee handbook or other set of standard policies

SANCTIONS

POLICY

Workforce members who violate the information security policies of the Company will be disciplined in proportion to the severity of the infraction.

PROCEDURE

1. Workforce members who are employees of the Company will be informed that compliance with the Company's information security policies is an essential function of the job. Employees who violate the security policies, either deliberately or unintentionally, are subject to discipline, up to and including termination. The appropriate disciplinary sanction for breach of information security policies will be decided on a case-by-case basis, depending on the severity of the violation, whether or not the violation was intentional, and the harm (if any) caused by the violation.

2. Workforce members who are not employees, but who have privileges to utilize the Company's information system, will be informed that they may lose such privileges if they violate information security policies, either intentionally or unintentionally. The appropriate sanction for breach of information security policies will be decided on a case-by-case basis, depending on the severity of the violation, whether or not the violation was intentional, and the harm (if any) caused by the violation.

REFERENCES
45 C.F.R. § 164.308(a)(1)(ii)(C)

3.2 ADOPT A BREACH NOTIFICATION POLICY

You should adopt a written policy to provide guidance to (1) determine when an impermissible use or disclosure of PHI constitutes a breach, (2) provide notification to individuals whose PHI is affected by the breach, and (3) report the breach to OCR. In addition to the sample policy that follows, add any requirements that would apply to you under state law for reporting of breaches of PHI, or of types of information that may be contained in PHI (such as social security numbers, account numbers, and other information that could be used for identity theft).

Make sure that your employees and non-employed workforce members receive training on promptly reporting a potential breach to the Security Official.

DOCUMENT 3D: BREACH NOTIFICATION POLICY

POLICY

If unsecured PHI is acquired, accessed, used or disclosed in a manner not permitted under the Health Insurance Portability and Accountability Act (HIPAA) Privacy Standards which compromises the security or privacy of the PHI, the Company will notify the individual whose PHI was affected, and the U.S. Department of Health and Human Services (HHS).

PROCEDURE

1. Definitions

    Breach means the acquisition, access, use, or disclosure of PHI in a manner not permitted under the HIPAA Privacy Standards, which compromises the security or privacy of the PHI. Certain unintentional incidents do not constitute a breach, as described in Section 3.

    Protected Health Information or *PHI* means information that (i) is created or received by a health care provider, health plan, employer, or health care clearinghouse; (ii) relates to the past, present, or future physical or mental health or condition of an individual; the provision of health care to an individual; or the past, present or future payment for the provision of health care to an individual; and (iii) that identifies the individual, or provides a reasonable basis to identify the individual. PHI does not include employment records held by the Company in its capacity as an employer, or information that has been deidentified in accordance with the HIPAA Privacy Standards.

    Unsecured PHI means PHI that has not been rendered unusable, unreadable or indecipherable to persons who are not authorized to access it, by shredding or destruction (in the case of paper, film or other hard copy media); or in the case of electronic records, by clearing, purging or destruction of electronic media in accordance with guidance of the National Institute for Standards and Technology (NIST), or encrypted in accordance with valid encryption processes recognized by the NIST.

2. Reporting of Known or Suspected Breach

   A. Any employee, workforce member or agent who discovers a potential breach shall report it to the Security Official of the Company.

   B. Subcontractors of the Company shall be required to report a suspected breach to the Security Official.

   C. If the Company discovers a breach involving PHI of one or more covered entities with which the Company has a business associate agreement, the Company shall report it to the covered entity in accordance with the business associate agreement.

3. Investigation of Suspected Breach

   A. The Security Official shall review the circumstances of the suspected breach to determine if the incident was intentional or unintentional.

      1. If PHI was acquired, accessed or used by a workforce member or agent of the Company or a business associate, but the acquisition, access or use was made in good faith and within the scope of permitted activities of the workforce member/agent, and there is no further unpermitted use or disclosure, then this does not constitute a breach.

         Example: An employee accessed the wrong record, but when he/she realized the error, the employee closed the record and did not retain any information.

      2. If PHI was inadvertently disclosed by one workforce member or agent of the Company to another workforce member/agent, and there is no further unpermitted use or disclosure, then this does not constitute a breach.

         Example: PHI of patients of covered entity A is disclosed to an employee who only provides services for covered entity B. The employee does not use or further disclose the information and reports the error.

3. If PHI was inadvertently disclosed, but the unauthorized person would not reasonably have been able to retain the information.

B. Except for the situations listed in subsection A, an impermissible use or disclosure of PHI is presumed to be a breach unless it can be demonstrated that there is a low probability that the PHI has been compromised. This determination shall be based on a risk assessment including at least the following factors:

- The nature and extent of the PHI involved, including the types of identifiers and the likelihood of re-identification
- The unauthorized person who used the PHI or to whom the disclosure was made
- Whether the PHI was actually acquired or viewed
- The extent to which the risk to the PHI has been mitigated.

The risk assessment shall be documented. If the risk assessment results in a conclusion that PHI may have been compromised, notification will be made as described below.

4. Breach Notification to Individuals

A. Written notice.

1. If there has been a breach of PHI that may have caused the PHI to be compromised, the individual will be notified in writing. The Company will coordinate notification with the covered entity so that individuals do not receive duplicate notification from both the Company and the covered entity
2. Notification will be sent without unreasonable delay, but in no event later than 60 days after discovery of the breach. EXCEPTION: If the Company has been notified by a law enforcement official that notification would impede a criminal investigation, notification will be delayed and the reason documented.
3. Notice will be sent to the individual's last known address by first class mail. If the individual had agreed

in advance to receive notice electronically, notice may be given by email.

    4.   The notice will contain the following information:
- A brief description of what happened
- A description of the types of unsecured PHI involved in the breach
- Any steps the individual should take to protect him/herself from potential harm resulting from the breach
- A brief description of steps the Company is taking to investigate the breach, to mitigate harm to individuals, and to protect against future breaches
- Contact procedures for the individual to ask questions, including a toll-free telephone number, an e-mail address, Web site or postal address.

    B.   Substitute notice.

        1.   If contact information for the individual is out-of-date, substitute notice will be given in a way reasonably calculated to reach the individual.

        2.   If there is insufficient contact information for ten or more individuals, then substitute notice will either be posted on the home page of the Hospital's website, or notice will be conveyed through major print or broadcast media.

    C.   Urgent notice. If there is danger of imminent misuse of the unsecured PHI, the individual will be notified by telephone or other means in addition to written notice.

5.   <u>Publication</u>

If a breach of unsecured PHI involves 500 or more residents of any state, then in addition to notifying the affected individuals, the Company will notify prominent media outlets in the state. The information conveyed will include the information required for individual notices.

6.   <u>Notice to HHS</u>

A. If a breach of unsecured PHI involves 500 or more individuals, the Company will notify HHS at the same time as notice is given to individuals.

B. For breach incidents involving fewer than 500 individuals, the Company will maintain a log of breach incidents and report to HHS not later than 60 days after the end of each calendar year.

3.3 ADOPT A POLICY ON COMPLIANCE WITH THE PRIVACY RULE, INCLUDING THE MINIMUM NECESSARY STANDARD

While some provisions of the Privacy Rule apply only to covered entities, business associates are prohibited from using or disclosing PHI in violation of the Privacy Rule, and must request, use and disclose only the minimum necessary PHI required to perform their function. Application of the minimum necessary rule is very fact-specific. For example, while a business associate that assists health plans with utilization review may require access to the entire medical record, a collection agency will only need access to billing information.

The following document is a sample policy on Privacy Rule compliance. Once again, it is critical that you provide training to your workforce on the requirements of the policy.

DOCUMENT 3E: POLICY ON COMPLIANCE WITH THE PRIVACY RULE

POLICY

The Company will use or disclose Protected Health Information (PHI) only as permitted under the HIPAA Privacy Rule. The Company will use or disclose only that PHI which is the minimum necessary required to perform its services, and will limit requests for PHI to the minimum necessary.

PROCEDURE

1. Employees and workforce members of the Company may not use or disclose PHI if the use or disclosure would violate the Privacy Rule, or would not be permitted under the Company's business associate agreement.

2. Employees and workforce members who need access to PHI to perform their job function will request and use only the minimum necessary to accomplish the task.

3. When disclosure of PHI is needed to perform the services provided by the Company, only the minimum necessary will be disclosed.

Step 4: Start Your Engines

4.1 Staff Training

All of your employees and other workforce members who have access to PHI should receive training on protecting the confidentiality and security of this information. The Security Standards require that every employee and other workforce member must receive training on implementation of the HIPAA Security Standards, and the policies that the Company has adopted to support compliance with the standards.

Document 4 is a training presentation, including notes for the presenter. It is probably most effective to present the information in person. If time constraints prevent this, have persons who cannot attend training review the presentation and confirm the completion of training in writing. Remember to record when each workforce member completed the training. Retain documentation of the date each employee/workforce member completed training for at least six years.

DOCUMENT 4A: STAFF TRAINING

Slide 1

Notes

• HIPAA stands for the "Health Insurance Portability and Accountability Act." The main purpose of this law was to allow people to change jobs without losing insurance coverage. Before HIPAA, when a person became covered under a new group health insurance plan, in many cases there were limits on coverage of preexisting conditions, and other limitations.

• HIPAA also included "Administrative Simplification" provisions. The goal of these provisions was to make processing of health care insurance claims more efficient, and save on administrative costs.

- HIPAA required health insurance companies to accept health care claims in a standard electronic format. So the first part of the HIPAA rules listed nine types of "standard transactions", and specified what data was required for each.

- However, privacy advocates worried that with more health care data becoming electronic, there would be a greater risks to the confidentiality of this information. Therefore, HIPAA also required the Department of Health and Human Services to adopt rules to protect health care information. Compliance with the HIPAA Privacy Rule was required starting in 2003, followed in 2005 by the Security Rule.

Slide 2

HIPAA Privacy

- The HIPAA Privacy Rule requires us to protect the confidentiality of all Protected Health Information (PHI), both paper and electronic
- Privacy safeguards
  - Protecting confidentiality is a basic element of the job for each of us.
  - We do not disclose PHI without proper authorization, or as permitted by law.
  - We request or use only the minimum necessary PHI.

Notes

• The HIPAA Privacy Rule required health care providers who submitted claims electronically, or used any of the other standard electronic transactions, to adopt procedures to guard "Protected Health Information" from improper disclosure, and to allow individuals access to their Protected Health Information. Protected Health Information includes not only information on the individual's diagnosis and treatment, but also any information that indicates the person is a patient, like name and address in connection with a health care provider or treatment.

Slide 3

The HIPAA Security Rule requires us to protect the
- Confidentiality
- Integrity
- Availability

Of Electronic Protected Health Information (EPHI)

HIPAA Security

Notes

• "Electronic Protected Health Information" is Protected Health Information that is stored in electronic media (like computer memory), or transmitted electronically (such as, over the Internet).

• In addition to protecting confidentiality, the Security Rule also requires us to protect data integrity (that is, to protect an individual's information from being altered inappropriately), and availability (to make sure the data is there when we need it to provide services).

• The Security Standards require us to analyze how we protect our electronic patient information, and take reasonable steps to enhance security.

• We also must adopt policies so that all employees and workforce members of the Company understand their role in protecting Protected Health Information.

Slide 4

- The HIPAA Security Rule requires that a single person be responsible for our information security management program.
- Our Security Official: (insert name and contact information)

Security Official

Notes

- The HIPAA Security Rules require that a single person be responsible for our information security management program. Our Security Official is (insert name and contact information).

- Our Security Official will review our information system according to the procedures required under HIPAA Security.

- The Security Official will also be responsible for updating our policies as our system changes, and keeping us informed about what we need to do to protect the security of our electronic protected health information.

Slide 5

- Password security
- Protection from viruses, worms, etc.
- Rules for Internet use
- Rules for email use
- Workstation safeguards
- Rules for portable media (CDs, USB drives, etc.)
- Rules for portable devices (laptops, tablets, smartphones)
- Downtime procedures
- Reporting of security incidents

Basic Security Safeguards

Notes

• Password security: Keep your password confidential!

• Protection from viruses: Make sure you don't introduce viruses or worms into our system by loading programs from home, opening unfamiliar email, or through the Internet.

• Workstation safeguards: Make sure only authorized users have access to workstations, and that PHI does not remain in plain sight on the screen when you are not at your workstation.

• Portable media: We should always know where our electronic PHI is.

• Security incidents: Promptly report any security incident to the Security Official. For example, this includes:

- Anytime someone tries to access PHI that he/she is not authorized to see;

- Any system "bug" or other problem that causes data to be unavailable or reported incorrectly;

- Any loss of PHI.

Slide 6

- DO NOT SHARE PASSWORDS!
- Change your password when required.
- Password selection:
  - Choose a password that you can remember, but that would be difficult for anyone else to guess.
  - Do not use "password", "1234", or repeating numbers or letters
  - Combine upper case and lower case letters, numbers, and special characters
  - If you must write down your password, keep it in a place where it cannot be easily found.

Password Security

Notes

• REMEMBER THAT YOUR PASSWORD MUST BE CONFIDENTIAL! Even if it may be cumbersome not to share your password with a coworker, you need to keep it confidential so that we can track system use according to the HIPAA Security Rule.

DO NOT:

• Post your password on your workstation or desk, or a bulletin board

• Tell your coworkers your password

• Use anyone else's password.

• If data needs to be accessed when you are not in the office, this does not usually require you to share your password. The office manager or Security Official should be able to reset the system. If it is absolutely necessary for you to let an authorized person know your password to access data in an emergency, then report this later to the Security Official, and reset your password when you return to the office.

• Reset your password when the system prompts you to do so, or at least every _____ months.

• [Review any special system requirements for passwords (e.g., minimum number of characters].

Slide 7

- Do not load software from home on your office computer.
- Follow rules for Internet use and email use:
  - Do not open an email or email attachment from an unknown source
  - Do not click on pop-up ads
  - Do not disable any security warnings
  - Follow security alerts from the Security Official.

Protection from viruses, worms, Trojans, etc.

Notes

• Do not bring any software from home to load on your office computer.

• Do not load any software until it is approved by the Security Official.

• Email must be used only for Company business. Keep personal emails to a minimum. Remember, the Company has the right to audit use of email.

• Do not open emails or an email attachment from an unknown source. If you receive suspicious emails, report them to the Security Official.

• The Security Official will stay informed about new viruses and worms that are a threat to information systems. If you receive any alert from the Security Official telling you to watch out for emails with a particular message or tagline, make sure to follow these. Let the Security Official know if you receive any such messages.

- Your Internet access is to be used for Company business. Keep personal use of the Internet to a minimum. Remember, the Company has the right to audit use of the Internet.

Slide 8

- Be sure to log off the system when you will be away from your work and when you leave for the day.
- Use screensavers when your computer is idle.
- Use a screening device if necessary to prevent unauthorized persons from viewing confidential information.

Workstation Safeguards

Notes

• [Describe any automatic log-off features of the systems (e.g., workstations are set to automatically log the user off after ___ minutes of inactivity.)]

• If you do not log off the system when you leave your workstation, any other person could see the PHI that you have access to, and enter data just as you could. In the system audit logs, it would appear that you had accessed or entered the data. So be sure to log off when you will be away from your workstation for more than a brief period.

• Make sure that the information on your monitor is not visible to persons walking by, etc. Position your computer monitor so that it is not easily viewed by outsiders, or if necessary, use a screening device so that it cannot be viewed except by the person using the computer. If you think any changes are needed, talk to your supervisor.

Slide 9

> - Do not copy confidential information to a CD or USB drive unless you get permission from the Security Official.
> - Do not take confidential information home unless you get permission from the Security Official.
>
> **Rules for Portable Media**

- PHI should not be copied to a CD or USB drive except as part of approved backup procedures.

Slide 10

- Protect against loss or theft of mobile devices
- Encrypt PHI on mobile devices
- Enable remote wipe of data
- Minimize storage of PHI on mobile devices, and backup
- Do not use unsecure WI-FI. Use a secure browser connection or a Virtual Private Network (VPN).

Rules for Mobile Devices

Notes

• If you use a laptop, smartphone, tablet PC or other portable electronic device to access PHI, make sure you are familiar with and use the security features of the device. If you lose the device, or it is stolen, you do not want outside parties to have access to your information. Contact the Security Official if you have questions about how to secure data on your portable device by encryption and other security features.

Slide 11

Examples of security incidents:
- Any attempt by an outsider to view, use, destroy or modify the Company's electronic information
- "Borrowing" passwords or other unauthorized use of a password
- Any attempt by an employee to access data that the employee does not have privileges to access
- Any interference with computer system operations

Security Incidents

Notes

• As part of his/her job, the Security Official will regularly check security features of the system and software and log unauthorized attempts to access information.

• The Security Official will investigate security incidents, and regularly update system security features and procedures.

• If For example, if you find out that someone has used your password, let the Security Official know.

Slide 12

- Promptly report any security incident to the Company's Security Official
- Do not use the system that is affected by the security incident. For example, if you suspect that hackers have gained access to the Company's email system, report by phone or in person.

Reporting Security Incidents

• Any security incident should be reported as promptly as possible.

• Provide instructions on how to report. IIf the Security Official is an outsourced IT person, provide address, phone number, email, etc.]

• [If you set up a hotline or similar function for HIPAA Security, describe how to access the hotline.]

Slide 13

Report any potential breach of PHI promptly to the Security Official. Examples:
- Misdirected fax
- Lost laptop
- Access to PHI by unauthorized party.

Breach of PHI

4.2 AMEND YOUR BUSINESS ASSOCIATE AGREEMENT

The standard Business Associate Agreement that you have been using may need to be amended, since the Privacy Rule and Security Rule provisions relating to business associate agreements have been modified in accordance with the HITECH Act. It is especially important that the business associate agreement state that the business associate will comply with applicable provisions of the Privacy Rule and the Security Rule, and will report any breach of unsecured PHI to the covered entity.

While the compliance date for the revised HIPAA rules is September 23, 2013, covered entities and business associates have an additional year to renegotiate existing business associate agreements to comply with the new rules.

The following document contains model Business Associate Agreement provisions that have been published by the Office for Civil Rights. The OCR provides this sample agreement as an example to covered entities and business associates. It is not mandatory that this sample be used, although a Business Associate Agreement should contain all elements described. Be sure to modify these sample provisions to apply to your services.

Document 4B: Business Associate Agreement[1]

Sample Business Associate Agreement Provisions

Words or phrases contained in brackets are intended as either optional language or as instructions to the users of these sample provisions.

Definitions

Catch-all definition:

The following terms used in this Agreement shall have the same meaning as those terms in the HIPAA Rules: Breach, Data Aggregation, Designated Record Set, Disclosure, Health Care Operations, Individual, Minimum Necessary, Notice of Privacy Practices, Protected Health Information, Required By Law, Secretary, Security Incident, Subcontractor, Unsecured Protected Health Information, and Use.

Specific definitions:

> (a) <u>Business Associate</u>. "Business Associate" shall generally have the same meaning as the term "business associate" at 45 CFR 160.103, and in reference to the party to this agreement, shall mean [Insert Name of Business Associate].
>
> (b) <u>Covered Entity</u>. "Covered Entity" shall generally have the same meaning as the term "covered entity" at 45 CFR 160.103, and in reference to the party to this agreement, shall mean [Insert Name of Covered Entity].

---

[1] Source: U.S. Department of Health and Human Services, Office for Civil Rights, available at http://www.hhs.gov/ocr/privacy/hipaa/understanding/coveredentities/contractprov.html.

(c) <u>HIPAA Rules</u>. "HIPAA Rules" shall mean the Privacy, Security, Breach Notification, and Enforcement Rules at 45 CFR Part 160 and Part 164.

Obligations and Activities of Business Associate

Business Associate agrees to:

(a) Not use or disclose protected health information other than as permitted or required by the Agreement or as required by law;

(b) Use appropriate safeguards, and comply with Subpart C of 45 CFR Part 164 with respect to electronic protected health information, to prevent use or disclosure of protected health information other than as provided for by the Agreement;

(c) Report to covered entity any use or disclosure of protected health information not provided for by the Agreement of which it becomes aware, including breaches of unsecured protected health information as required at 45 CFR 164.410, and any security incident of which it becomes aware;

[The parties may wish to add additional specificity regarding the breach notification obligations of the business associate, such as a stricter timeframe for the business associate to report a potential breach to the covered entity and/or whether the business associate will handle breach notifications to individuals, the HHS Office for Civil Rights (OCR), and potentially the media, on behalf of the covered entity.]

(d) In accordance with 45 CFR 164.502(e)(1)(ii) and 164.308(b)(2), if applicable, ensure that any subcontractors that create, receive, maintain, or transmit protected health information on behalf of the business associate agree to the same restrictions, conditions, and requirements that apply to the business associate with respect to such information;

(e) Make available protected health information in a designated record set to the [Choose either "covered entity" or "individual or the individual's designee"] as necessary to satisfy covered entity's obligations under 45 CFR 164.524;

[The parties may wish to add additional specificity regarding how the business associate will respond to a request for access that the business associate receives directly from the individual (such as whether and in what time and manner a business associate is to provide the requested access or whether the business associate will forward the individual's request to the covered entity to fulfill) and the timeframe for the business associate to provide the information to the covered entity.]

(f) Make any amendment(s) to protected health information in a designated record set as directed or agreed to by the covered entity pursuant to 45 CFR 164.526, or take other measures as necessary to satisfy covered entity's obligations under 45 CFR 164.526;

[The parties may wish to add additional specificity regarding how the business associate will respond to a request for amendment that the business associate receives directly from the individual (such as whether and in what time and manner a business associate is to act on the request for amendment or whether the business associate will forward the individual's request to the covered entity) and the timeframe for the business associate to incorporate any amendments to the information in the designated record set.]

(g) Maintain and make available the information required to provide an accounting of disclosures to the [Choose either "covered entity" or "individual"] as necessary to satisfy covered entity's obligations under 45 CFR 164.528;

[The parties may wish to add additional specificity regarding how the business associate will respond to a request for an accounting of disclosures that the business associate receives directly from the individual (such as whether and in what time and manner the business associate is to provide the accounting of disclosures to the individual or whether the business associate will forward the request to the covered entity) and the timeframe for the business associate to provide information to the covered entity.]

(h) To the extent the business associate is to carry out one or more of covered entity's obligation(s) under Subpart E of 45 CFR Part 164, comply with the requirements of Subpart E that apply to the covered entity in the performance of such obligation(s); and

(i) Make its internal practices, books, and records available to the Secretary for purposes of determining compliance with the HIPAA Rules.

Permitted Uses and Disclosures by Business Associate

(a) Business associate may only use or disclose protected health information

[Option 1 – Provide a specific list of permissible purposes.]

[Option 2 – Reference an underlying service agreement, such as "as necessary to perform the services set forth in Service Agreement."]

[In addition to other permissible purposes, the parties should specify whether the business associate is authorized to use protected health information to de-identify the information in accordance with 45 CFR 164.514(a)-(c). The parties also may wish to specify the manner in which the business associate will de-identify the information and the permitted uses and disclosures by the business associate of the de-identified information.]

(b) Business associate may use or disclose protected health information as required by law.

(c) Business associate agrees to make uses and disclosures and requests for protected health information

[Option 1] consistent with covered entity's minimum necessary policies and procedures.

[Option 2] subject to the following minimum necessary requirements: [Include specific minimum necessary provisions that are consistent with the covered entity's minimum necessary policies and procedures.]

(d) Business associate may not use or disclose protected health information in a manner that would violate Subpart E of 45 CFR Part 164 if done by covered entity [if the Agreement permits the business associate to use or disclose protected health information for its own management and administration and legal responsibilities or for data aggregation services as set forth in optional provisions (e), (f), or (g) below, then add ", except for the specific uses and disclosures set forth below."]

(e) [Optional] Business associate may use protected health information for the proper management and administration of the business associate or to carry out the legal responsibilities of the business associate.

(f) [Optional] Business associate may disclose protected health information for the proper management and administration of business associate or to carry out the legal responsibilities of the business associate, provided the disclosures are required by law, or business associate obtains reasonable assurances from the person to whom the information is disclosed that the information will remain confidential and used or further disclosed only as required by law or for the purposes for which it was disclosed to the person, and the person notifies business associate of any instances of which it is aware in which the confidentiality of the information has been breached.

(g) [Optional] Business associate may provide data aggregation services relating to the health care operations of the covered entity.

Provisions for Covered Entity to Inform Business Associate of Privacy Practices and Restrictions

(a) [Optional] Covered entity shall notify business associate of any limitation(s) in the notice of privacy practices of covered entity under 45 CFR 164.520, to the extent that such limitation may affect business associate's use or disclosure of protected health information.

(b) [Optional] Covered entity shall notify business associate of any changes in, or revocation of, the permission by an individual to use or disclose his or her protected health information, to the extent that such changes may affect business associate's use or disclosure of protected health information.

(c) [Optional] Covered entity shall notify business associate of any restriction on the use or disclosure of protected health information that covered entity has agreed to or is required to abide by under 45 CFR 164.522, to the extent that such restriction may affect business associate's use or disclosure of protected health information.

Permissible Requests by Covered Entity

[Optional] Covered entity shall not request business associate to use or disclose protected health information in any manner that would not be permissible under Subpart E of 45 CFR Part 164 if done by covered entity. [Include an exception if the business associate will use or disclose protected health information for, and the agreement includes provisions for, data aggregation or management and administration and legal responsibilities of the business associate.]

Term and Termination

(a) Term. The Term of this Agreement shall be effective as of [Insert effective date], and shall terminate on [Insert termination date or event] or on the date covered entity terminates for cause as authorized in paragraph (b) of this Section, whichever is sooner.

(b) Termination for Cause. Business associate authorizes termination of this Agreement by covered entity, if covered entity determines business associate has violated a material term of the Agreement [and business associate has not cured the breach or ended the violation within the time specified by covered entity]. [Bracketed language may be added if the covered entity wishes to provide the business associate with an opportunity to cure a violation or breach of the contract before termination for cause.]

(c) Obligations of Business Associate Upon Termination.

[Option 1 – if the business associate is to return or destroy all protected health information upon termination of the agreement]

Upon termination of this Agreement for any reason, business associate shall return to covered entity [or, if agreed to by covered entity, destroy] all protected health information received from covered entity, or created, maintained, or received by business associate on behalf of covered entity, that the business associate still maintains in any form. Business associate shall retain no copies of the protected health information.

[Option 2—if the agreement authorizes the business associate to use or disclose protected health information for its own management and administration or to carry out its legal responsibilities and the business associate needs to retain protected health information for such purposes after termination of the agreement]

Upon termination of this Agreement for any reason, business associate, with respect to protected health information received from covered entity, or created, maintained, or received by business associate on behalf of covered entity, shall:

1. Retain only that protected health information which is necessary for business associate to continue its proper management and administration or to carry out its legal responsibilities;
2. Return to covered entity [or, if agreed to by covered entity, destroy] the remaining protected health information that the business associate still maintains in any form;
3. Continue to use appropriate safeguards and comply with Subpart C of 45 CFR Part 164 with respect to electronic protected health information to prevent use or disclosure of the protected health information, other than as provided for in this Section, for as long as business associate retains the protected health information;
4. Not use or disclose the protected health information retained by business associate other than for the purposes for which such protected health information

was retained and subject to the same conditions set out at [Insert section number related to paragraphs (e) and (f) above under "Permitted Uses and Disclosures By Business Associate"] which applied prior to termination; and

5. Return to covered entity [or, if agreed to by covered entity, destroy] the protected health information retained by business associate when it is no longer needed by business associate for its proper management and administration or to carry out its legal responsibilities.

[The agreement also could provide that the business associate will transmit the protected health information to another business associate of the covered entity at termination, and/or could add terms regarding a business associate's obligations to obtain or ensure the destruction of protected health information created, received, or maintained by subcontractors.]

(d) <u>Survival</u>. The obligations of business associate under this Section shall survive the termination of this Agreement.

Miscellaneous [Optional]

(a) [Optional] <u>Regulatory References</u>. A reference in this Agreement to a section in the HIPAA Rules means the section as in effect or as amended.

(b) [Optional] <u>Amendment</u>. The Parties agree to take such action as is necessary to amend this Agreement from time to time as is necessary for compliance with the requirements of the HIPAA Rules and any other applicable law.

(c) [Optional] <u>Interpretation</u>. Any ambiguity in this Agreement shall be interpreted to permit compliance with the HIPAA Rules.

While you will need to use a Business Associate Agreement complying with the HITECH Act and the final rules for new business relationships with covered entities, it may be easier for you to amend the business associate agreements that you now have in force. The following document is a draft amendment that you can use with existing clients. This contains only the new obligations imposed on business associates under HITECH, assuming that your existing Business Associate Agreement complied with the original Privacy Rule.

Document 4C: Business Associate Agreement Amendment

Amendment to Business Associate Agreement

Recitals

(a) [Insert name of your client] ("Client") and [insert name of your company] ("Business Associate") entered into a Business Associate Agreement (the "Agreement") effective [insert date of original Business Associate Agreement] to provide for the protection of Protected Health Information ("PHI") entrusted to Business Associate by Client.

(b) The Health Information Technology for Economic and Clinical Health (HITECH) Act (the "Act"), and regulations of the Department of Health and Human Services implementing the Act, require that the Agreement be amended to reflect responsibilities of Business Associate pursuant to the Act.

Agreement

1. Business Associate shall use appropriate safeguards, and comply with Subpart C of 45 CFR Part 164 with respect to electronic protected health information, to prevent use or disclosure of protected health information other than as provided for by the Agreement.
2. Business Associate shall report to Client any use or disclosure of protected health information not provided for by the Agreement of which it becomes aware, including breaches of unsecured protected health information as required at 45 CFR 164.410, and any security incident of which it becomes aware.
3. To the extent the Business Associate is to carry out one or more of Client's obligation(s) as a covered entity under Subpart E of 45 CFR Part 164, Business Associate shall comply with the

requirements of Subpart E that apply to the covered entity in the performance of such obligation(s).
4. This Amendment shall take effect when signed by both parties.

COVERED ENTITY (CLIENT)   **BUSINESS ASSOCIATE**

By:_____   By:_____

Print name:_____   Print name:_____

Title:_____   Title:_____

Date:_____   Date:_____

4.3 Amend Your Agreements With Subcontractors

Now, subcontractors of business associates are also required to comply with the Security Rule and relevant provisions of the Privacy Rule, just as business associates are. You must have written agreements with all subcontractors that handle PHI, that specify the subcontractors will observe the same restrictions on use and disclosure of PHI that apply to you as a business associate. Again, a year is allowed to complete renegotiation of these agreements.

STEP 5: HANDLING BUMPS IN THE ROAD

5.1 SECURITY INCIDENTS AND BREACHES

As indicated in the policies above, the Security Official will be responsible for investigating all security incidents. Security incidents may be reported by workforce members, or uncovered through the Security Official's monitoring activities. All security incidents must be documented, whether they involve temporary loss of availability of PHI, unauthorized modification of PHI, or possible inappropriate use or disclosure.

Security incidents that involve possible inappropriate use or disclosure of PHI must also be reviewed to determine whether they constitute reportable breaches of unsecured PHI, in accordance with the Breach Notification Policy.

Document 5 is a template for recording the reporting and investigation of security incidents, and recording remedial action.

Document 5: Security Incident Report

The Security Official is responsible for investigating any security incident, to determine the root cause and identify measures that can prevent such incidents in the future. A security incident occurs when there is any actual improper disclosure of, loss of, or alteration of electronic patient information. An unsuccessful attempt to gain improper access to electronic patient information is also a security incident.

Security incidents can range from minor issues that do not result in actual loss of data (such as unexpected system downtime) to major issues such as theft of a laptop containing PHI, or employee dishonesty. The form below can be used for documentation of minor issues. If a major security incident occurs, a complete root cause analysis must be done to identify the source and scope of the problem.

Date of incident	Date of report	Nature of incident	Source of report	Findings	Corrective Action

Appendix A: Other Resources

The checklists, policies and other documents contained in *The HIPAA Roadmap for Business Associates* are available as Word documents, and the training presentation as a PowerPoint, at www.digitalagemd.com.

For more information from governmental sources, see the following:

HIPAA Omnibus Final Rule, 78 Fed. Reg. 5566 (Jan. 25, 2013).

U.S. Department of Health and Human Services, Office for Civil Rights, http://www.hhs.gov/ocr/privacy/index.html

National Institute of Standards and Technology (NIST), Computer Security Resource Center, http://csrc.nist.gov/

    NIST HIPAA Security Rule Toolkit: http://scap.nist.gov/hipaa/

    NIST Special Publication 800-66, *An Introductory Resource Guide for Implementing the Health Insurance Portability and Accountability Act (HIPAA) Security Rule,* Revision 1.

Appendix B: Definitions

1. Access means the ability or the means necessary to read, write, modify, or communicate data or information, or otherwise use any resource of the Company's record systems relating to Protected Health Information (including medical information and patient account information) which is stored or transmitted using electronic media.

2. Authentication means the corroboration that a person is the one claimed. This includes written and electronic signature of entries according to the Company's policies, and other means of identifying a person who writes or modifies Protected Health Information.

3. Electronic media means:
   (a) Electronic storage media, including memory devices in computers (i.e., hard drives) and any removable/transportable digital memory medium, such as magnetic tape or disk, optical disk, USB drive or digital memory card; or
   (b) Transmission media used to exchange information already in electronic storage media. Transmission media include, for example, the internet (wide-open); extranet (using internet technology to link a business with information accessible only to collaborating parties); leased lines; dial-up lines; private networks; and the physical movement of removable/transportable electronic storage media.
   When information has not been in electronic form before transmission (e.g., paper or voice information), the information is not electronic. This includes paper-to-paper faxes, person-to-person telephone calls, video conferencing, or voicemail messages.

4. Electronic protected health information means protected health information which is maintained in or transmitted by electronic media.

5. Encryption means the use of an algorithmic process to transform data into a form in which there is a low probability of assigning meaning without use of a confidential process or key.

6. Information system means an interconnected set of information resources under the same direct management control that shares common functionality. The Company's information system includes its server, desktop computers, laptops, smartphones, software, and other related systems, data and resources.

7. Integrity means the property that data or information have not been altered or destroyed in an unauthorized manner.

8. Security Incident means any attempt at unauthorized access, use, disclosure, modification, or destruction of information, or interference with system operations in the information system. Such an attempt is a security incident, whether or not the attempt is successful.

About the author

Patricia D. King, J.D., M.B.A. is a health care attorney based in the Chicago area. She has over 30 years of experience representing health care providers, including community hospitals, academic medical centers, multispecialty physician groups and provider-owned insurance entities.

Pat has had a long-term interest in health information technology, including privacy and security of electronic health records, HIPAA compliance, health information exchange, and mhealth. She is a Vice Chair of the Health Information and Technology Practice Group of the American Health Lawyers Association, and a member of the Legal Task Force of HIMSS.

Pat is a graduate of the University of Wisconsin Law School and the University of Chicago Booth School of Business.

Made in the USA
San Bernardino, CA
15 April 2015